Glenn Goldsmith

# *Silver Burdett Picture Histories*

# The Age of Discovery

## *1450 – 1600*

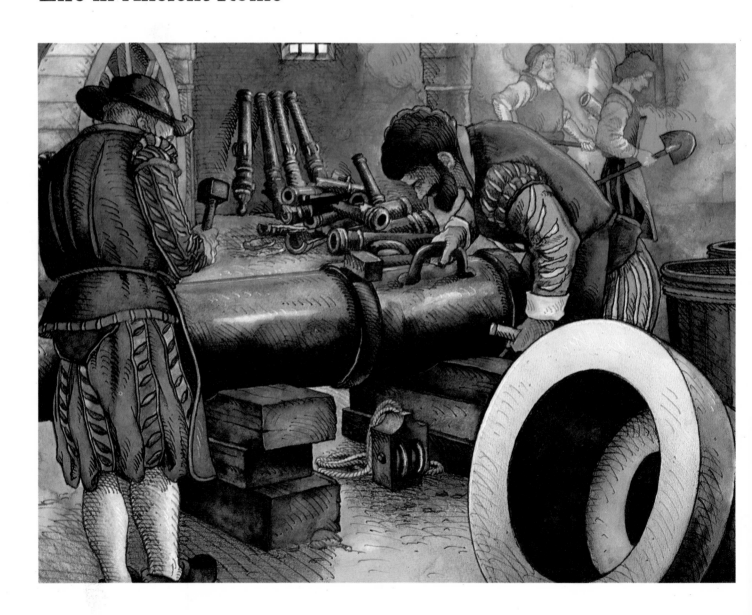

# Silver Burdett Picture Histories

# The Age of Discovery

**Pierre Miquel**
**Illustrated by Claude and Denise Millet**

Translated and adapted by Peter Furtado
from La Vie privée des Hommes: Au temps des grandes découvertes
first published in France in 1976 by
Librairie Hachette, Paris

Published in the United States by
Silver Burdett Company, Morristown, N.J.
1981 Printing

ISBN 0-382-06474-7

Library of Congress Catalog Card No. 80-52500

# Contents

# Introduction

All through the Middle Ages, Europe had been shut in on itself. The Mediterranean was the centre of the medieval world. Everything revolved around Rome and the other cities of Italy; England was considered to be almost on the very edge of the world. The Church, ruled over by the Pope, had real power over every person in Europe and could control the destinies of kings and kingdoms. The power of the Church held Europe, or Christendom as it was known, more unified than it would ever be again. For, as well as wielding political power, the Church ruled over men's minds. Every thinker and every artist worked for the Church; the Church's ideas about the world, about the universe, about society and about life went unchallenged. The medieval European had little sense of adventure or discovery, little desire to find out anything outside the world he knew. The only other civilization in regular contact with Europeans was that of the Turks – a civilization the Europeans repeatedly tried to destroy in the Crusades. Even the Crusades were simply military expeditions to restore Jerusalem to what the Europeans considered to be its rightful place at the centre of Christendom. The Crusaders had no dream of discovery in their hearts.

In the 15th century all this began to change. Scholars and artists were the first to experience this change: they discovered the history and the art of the ancient Greeks and Romans. As they found out more about these great achievements and read the works of the men who made them, these scholars began to question many of their own assumptions about the world. At first they replaced the styles of medieval art with copies of the Roman; but soon they questioned the whole system of ideas on which life in medieval Christendom was based. By studying the history of the Roman Republic and Empire, the scholars discovered new ideas about politics and society. At first, they tried to copy the ways and behaviour of ancient Rome – especially in the small, rich city-states of Italy – but soon people actually started to think for themselves.

Science was one important field where this wind of change was felt. Many important discoveries were made in the basic fields of science – astronomy, physics and medicine. But an even greater achievement was the discovery of the method by which scientists ought to work: men like Galileo, Vesalius, and Bacon all realized that the scientist's main job is to be continually observing; to be watching, looking at nature and wondering about it then the scientist must experiment to see if his ideas are right. No longer were scientists relying on the work of men many centuries ago; they were devising detailed experiments to see if their ideas were correct. This basic method of work was to lead to great achievements. Men began to discover the natural world: they confirmed that the Earth goes round the Sun, and they began to understand how the human body works. They dreamed up new tools of industry and devices to help the navigators sailing for weeks out of sight of land.

For, suddenly, Europeans were seized with the desire to discover more of the world than they had ever known before. They were encouraged by the fact that trading with the East by the overland route was now extremely expensive since the Turks demanded high taxes to allow the goods to pass. But instead of launching yet another Crusade against the Turks, the Portuguese decided to explore the possibilities of sailing around Africa to reach India and China. Even more remarkable, Christopher Columbus acted on his idea (which everyone else thought mad) to sail west to reach China. He did not succeed, but neither did he fall off the edge of the world as people expected; instead he discovered the landmass of America. Soon Portugal and Spain became hugely rich from the achievements of their discoverers; in the East, the Portuguese found there were fortunes to be won from trading in luxury goods, especially spices, and in the Americas, there were the fabulously wealthy empires of the Incas and Aztecs to be conquered by a handful of Spaniards armed with a few guns. Europe was soon filled with this treasure, and the world was changed for ever.

Now it was the Atlantic and not the Mediterranean that was the centre of Europe's prosperity. The change was important for the future. Countries like England, France, the still-united state of Belgium and Holland, and the Holy Roman Empire (which covered a vast area that included modern Germany, Austria, Switzerland and north Italy) all had easier access to the shipping routes of the Atlantic than had the old trading capitals of Florence and Venice. These countries became wealthier and their mood more confident. Nevertheless, much of the political activity of Europe, the wars and the diplomatic dealing, still went on in Italy. The Italian cities, assisted by powerful allies, indulged in squabbles

**The Great Flocks of Sheep in Spain**
*Two and a half million sheep lived in Spain in the 16th century. They travelled north in summer and south in winter, devastating everything in their path.*

**Feudal Duties in Russia**
*If a Russian peasant in 1500 was granted two hectares of land to farm for himself, he had to farm about a hectare for his lord. By 1600, this obligation had more or less doubled.*

which proved a fertile ground for the diplomatic conflicts of the great monarchs. The 'Italian Wars' broke out in earnest and for over fifty years they affected all of Europe. They provided the main field of rivalry between Francis I, King of France, and his great enemy Charles V, the Holy Roman Emperor. Charles, after 1519, was ruler of more than half of Europe: he was king of the newly unified Spain, ruler of the Netherlands and king of Naples as well as emperor and ruler of the Spanish conquests in the New World. In the quarrels between these two men, with Henry VIII of England taking a third, less important, part, the national identities of their countries – Spain, France and England – were forged. For thirty years these three men manoeuvred and fought for advantages over each other. Their courts became more splendid and more costly, their wars more violent and their rule over their kingdoms more despotic. Charles had what seemed to be unlimited wealth from the New World at his disposal, but his empire was too unwieldy; Henry and Francis had more unified kingdoms, but had to reorganize the government and tax systems to finance their dreams. As they took their share of their countries' prosperity and concentrated their nations' glory in their own persons, so they re-examined the idea of kingship, and how a king may act.

The new thinking, and the discovery of national identity, gave rise to another great change. A movement attacking the abuses of the Church arose in the Holy Roman Empire in the 1520s. The movement soon developed into a complete attack on the authority of the Pope and certain doctrines of the Church. The Protestants, as the reformers were called, used the Bible as the foundation of their faith. All over Europe, princes and kings saw a chance to develop their hopes of national independence and to deny the power of the Pope. In the Holy Roman Empire, the princes of many regions rebelled against the Emperor

### Coal in England
*Not much coal was mined until 1550; but soon more than 200,000 tonnes a year were being dug up. The Midlands, Northumberland, Wales and Scotland were the main coal-mining areas.*

### Treasure from the New World
*Between 1558 and 1598, the king of Spain's income from gold and silver brought from his lands in America went up by over four times.*

### Textiles: A Successful Industry
*There were 30,000 members of the wool guild in Florence. Employers were very strict: workers clocked in in the morning and clocked out in the evening under the eyes of their foremen.*

*Five thousand men were employed in the silk industry of Lyon, 30,000 in Seville.*

and demanded the right to choose between the Roman Catholic Church and the reformers; in England Henry VIII, though disagreeing with the Protestants in many ways, took the opportunity to break with the Pope and declare himself head of the English Church.

The Bible, which had formerly been read in Latin, was translated into the everyday languages of Europe. Inspired by the books which poured from the new printing presses, people began to question their religion and form their own opinions about it. Above all, they put forward new answers to difficult questions of faith and challenged the power of the Catholic Church.

All the ideas that had held Europe together were falling apart, and in many places civil war occurred. The Catholics reformed their worst abuses and set about a counterattack against the Protestants, by education and by war. The political leader of this 'Counter-Reformation' was Philip II of Spain, son of Charles V and inheritor of most of his father's titles except that of Emperor. Protestantism had taken strongest hold over the merchant communities of northern Europe, especially in the Netherlands; Philip set out to restore Catholicism there by force. The Dutch resisted with a full-scale revolt against Spanish rule. They supported themselves by taking over much of the Portuguese trade in the Far East; and eventually they won their independence.

Philip's second great enemy was England. In 1554 he married the Catholic Queen Mary and helped her restore Catholicism. Mary was the eldest daughter of Henry VIII. Her mother was Henry's first wife, Catherine of Aragon, whom Henry divorced to marry Ann Boleyn. Mary succeeded her Protestant brother Edward in 1553. But after Mary's death, her younger sister, Elizabeth, re-established the Protestant Church in England. Eventually war broke out between England and Spain which reached its climax with the Spanish Armada invasion attempt of 1588. England survived, and the religious war emboldened her pirates to raid Spanish treasure fleets in the New World, and lay the foundations of future English naval power.

France, too, suffered a long and bloody religious war. Catherine de Medici, and her Catholic supporters faced a revolt by the Protestants or Huguenots, who lived mainly in the south and west of France. France lost much of her prestige during this civil war, and peace was eventually made in 1598, when Henry of Navarre, the Protestant heir to the French throne, finally converted to Catholicism.

Despite these upheavals, Europe's population was expanding fast, and Europe's prosperity, too. New industries flourished, but prices went up fast, and towns grew even faster; soon there were hordes of beggars all over the continent. Ways of dealing with the problems caused by economic expansion and industry remained to be discovered in the future.

In every way, Europeans were extending themselves. Printing made new ideas easily available to everyone who could read, and the whole age seemed to embody a spirit of discovery, both physically, in the exploration of the world, and intellectually, in the exploration of the mind. Because of this spirit of discovery, and what it achieved, the 16th century is often thought to mark the beginning of the modern age.

# Life in the Towns

**The towns were at the centre of all the great changes of the 16th century.** In the towns, men were free to make money, to spend their wealth in new ways, to meet people from other countries, to exchange new ideas and to think for themselves. The great towns of Europe were very large – Naples had a population of 230,000 in 1500, and Paris of 200,000. Both towns almost doubled in size by 1600. The great merchants in Italy dominated the towns, and were lavish supporters of the arts. The town councils also set about creating beautiful squares, open spaces and fine buildings. In Germany towns, such as Heidelberg, had famous universities which attracted students from all over Europe.

In England, only London could compare with these great European cities. It had about 60,000 inhabitants in 1500, and was the centre of the country's import trade from Europe, and for cloth exports. It was also the home of the Court and Parliament, and, in Elizabeth's reign, London became the home of the flourishing theatre of Shakespeare. It had become very crowded by 1600, and the city council tried in vain to control the activities of greedy landlords.

The other towns of England were far smaller: Norwich, the second largest, had only 13,000 people; Newcastle and Bristol had 10,000 each. Towns like these often had one great industry – cloth or fishing – but they housed many other trades too.

English towns had been generally small and poor since the Black Death of the 1350s but now they were beginning to grow again. But there was little money to spare for lavish projects of rebuilding – for some, like Boston in Lincolnshire, even the job of keeping the harbour open was too expensive, and so the town's export trade soon died. Houses were crowded together, with little light, no running water and no sewerage; conditions were very dirty. But even so, the rich and the poor, the fishwife and the tanner, the merchant and the journeyman were always coming into contact with one another – townlife was always exciting.

People put glass windows into their houses for the first time since the Romans in the mid-15th century. But glass was a great luxury, and if they ever moved they usually took the glass with them. People now used wealth on comfort.

Architects were still considered to be more like craftsmen or engineers than artists, and the names of very few English architects from the 16th century are known. In Italy, though, architecture was considered a great art, and architects were celebrated for their work.

At Tivoli, not far from Rome, the grounds of the Villa d'Este, which belonged to a great family of Modena, were laid out with a fine Renaissance garden. There were fountains, statues and cool terraces everywhere. Parks gradually became popular near all great cities.

An old, forgotten Egyptian obelisk was put up again in Rome in St Peter's Square. They had to move it only 250 metres, but the job took 130 days, 800 labourers and 150 horses. No city in England was able to afford such extravagance.

Roman ruins had been mostly ignored during the Middle Ages, but now they were explored and studied. Their designs and their proportions were copied by the new architects, who even took columns or sculptures from them to include into new buildings of their own.

# Merchant Princes

**All over Europe, merchants became the richest and most powerful men in the land.** The nobility and the Church still had great prestige and controlled vast estates, but neither could turn their wealth into cash very easily. The merchants were, therefore, in the best position to control the changing destinies of their countries. In many places, men made their fortunes from trading in cloth, or spices, or grain or wine. Then they expanded their activities into other goods, since the guilds, which had once kept all the various trades separate, no longer had much power. Eventually, these men reached the peak of their wealth by becoming bankers, to whom kings would turn when they needed the money to pay their armies, or to build a new palace, or pay for bribes.

In some places, such as the Italian cities, these merchant bankers became princes; members of the Medici family from Florence became (1) pope, (2) queen of France and (3) princes in Italy. In the Netherlands, the merchants went through a great struggle to gain their freedom from Spanish rule and they were inspired to abolish princes altogether and set up a republic. Others, like the immensely rich Fugger family in Germany, and Thomas Gresham in England, remained as financiers, but directed the money matters of their monarch from behind the scenes.

In many countries, however, the place of the merchants in society was not secure. In Spain, trade and business were so despised that the poorest noble considered himself far above any merchant – and as a result, the Spaniards failed to make good use of all the wealth that they imported from the New World. Even in England, the nobility enjoyed such high prestige that most merchants, after making their fortune, bought a great estate or married into a noble family. The idea that money should be used to make even more money, instead of spending it in magnificent banquets or castles, was still a new one – the Church even thought it was immoral. Nevertheless, like the new ideas that were being spread about in printed books, this idea too reached more and more people, and eventually changed completely the whole face of European society.

In order to keep an accurate tally of their money, merchants developed a new method of keeping accounts in the 14th century, known as double-entry book-keeping. It was now widely used, even for the royal finances, by careful kings such as Henry VII of England.

Bankers had to transport gold and silver bullion by road. There was always a danger of robbers, and as a result, they started using letters of credit, or cheques, instead of actual shipments of precious metals, and this system is still in use today.

These healthy-looking merchants are shown at the Exchange at Antwerp which was one of Europe's richest towns in 1500, and the main centre for trade in northern Europe. Its wealth was based on a trade in jewels, but at the Exchange, which was built in 1531, merchants came in search of cloth, wool, spices, luxury items, furs and corn, as well as to change money. Many merchants made money by buying and selling the currency of different states. Some currencies, though, like the Venetian ducat and the Dutch florin, were accepted by traders all over Europe.

Coins were made by hand. Each mint was responsible for making good coins, and every coin was measured. Henry VIII tried to cut down the amount of silver in the coins, in order to make himself richer – but he only put prices up.

Every town had its pawnbrokers and money lenders, who provided a valuable service for the poor, but made large profits. There were no private bank accounts, and so this was the only way to get a loan to start up in business.

# Fortune from the Sea

**Christopher Columbus, sailing under the Spanish flag, discovered the West Indies in 1492; Vasco da Gama, from Portugal, sailed all the way to India in 1498.** From then on, explorers in tiny ships, twenty to thirty metres long, and often away from home for several years at a time, completely changed the shape of the known world, opening up vast new empires. Nevertheless, many ships were lost, in storms off Cape Horn or exploring the icy seas to the north of Canada in search of a new route to China; and many explorers, like Columbus himself, did not live to find out the significance of their discoveries.

At first, England took part energetically, and her many excellent harbours, easy access to the Atlantic and experienced fishing fleets, gave her a strong advantage. In 1497, Henry VII sponsored John Cabot and his son to journey to North America; on that voyage they discovered Newfoundland. But for the next sixty years, the English concentrated on trade with Northern Europe, while the Spanish and Portuguese built up huge empires in South America.

The West Country – Bristol, Plymouth and Exeter in particular – saw the rise of a fine ship-building industry, and some solid private trading fleets. After the accession of Elizabeth, these towns became the centres from which the great sailors and explorers set out – men like Francis Drake, who raided the Spanish treasure ships and sailed right around the world in 1577–80; Walter Raleigh, who was the first to try to create a colony in North America, and brought back new crops like the potato and tobacco; or John Hawkins, who in 1562 sailed to West Africa, bought a shipload of slaves for a few trinkets, took them to the West Indies and sold them to the owners of the sugar plantations there. By doing this he set up the slave trade that made England the richest country in the world by 1800.

The Mediterranean had once been the hub of Europe's trade with the rest of the world. But it was now too dangerous. The Turks had a strong fleet of galleys in the east and allowed few traders through, and even in the west the Barbary pirates, who were based along the coasts of North Africa, raided any trading vessels. They stole the cargo, burnt the ship and sold the crew into slavery. The Turkish fleet was defeated at the battle of Lepanto in 1571, but the threat from the Barbary pirates continued until the beginning of the nineteenth century.

Francis Drake made his fortune from raiding Spanish galleons loaded with gold and silver from America. He gave some of this booty to Queen Elizabeth, who paid for part of his expenses. The English had no regular trade with other continents until 1600.

Galleys driven by oars were valuable in the Mediterranean, where there was no steady wind. Venice had a fleet of galleys that went as far as the Black Sea; but these boats were not strong enough to stand up to the Atlantic.

Devices for navigation were essential to ocean-going sailors. They used the astrolabe to work out the height of the sun or stars. From this they calculated their latitude. These complicated metal rings representing the longitude and latitude helped with these sums.

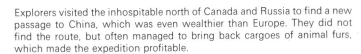

Explorers visited the inhospitable north of Canada and Russia to find a new passage to China, which was even wealthier than Europe. They did not find the route, but often managed to bring back cargoes of animal furs, which made the expedition profitable.

# Adventurers and Conquistadors

**When the Spaniards arrived on the mainland of America soon after 1500, they began to carve out huge empires.** There was already a fine Aztec civilization in Mexico, and an Inca one in Peru, but these people had no chance against the Europeans who carried firearms and were equipped with horses, which the Americans had never seen before. At first they thought these white men were gods, and the Spanish leaders made huge expeditions, conquering and stealing all that they could find. In Mexico, Hernan Cortés captured the Aztec emperor Montezuma by trickery and later took his capital city; in Peru, Francisco Pizarro cheated the Inca leader Atahualpa of a huge ransom, and then took all the Inca territory, in 1528–33. The Spaniards treated the natives with great cruelty and created vast estates for themselves with the Indians virtually as slaves. Many Indians were converted to Christianity (they were executed if they refused); but the Church did little to improve their conditions.

The Portuguese were more respectful of the cultures that they encountered. They built a series of strong forts along the coast of East Africa to protect their trade with India, and also claimed a small part of the Indian mainland, known as Goa, for themselves. But otherwise they were content to trade.

As the demand for spices increased in Europe, the Dutch seized control of the valuable Portuguese pepper trade with the East Indies. They then set up several colonies, in Java and Batavia, where they created vast factories for spices, and enslaved the population.

The English explorers were not yet so brutal; the early visitors to north America had friendly relations with the Indians there, although the first attempts to set up an English colony in Virginia in the 1580's were destroyed by Indian attacks. Then the English began to take African slaves to the West Indies – a trade which was to cause havoc to the cultures of central Africa. All in all, Europe treated the rest of the world extraordinarily badly in the 16th century.

Explorers found many animals on their travels that were undreamt of in medieval Europe. They also found people whose way of life was very different from the European. They wrote books about what they had seen, and often included many outlandish stories.

The Spanish founded a silver mine at Potosí, in Peru, one of the highest cities in the world. They forced the Indians to work in the mines, which became the richest source of silver ever. Many thousands died in the airless conditions underground.

The Spanish explorers, or conquistadors, in the New World of Central and South America were treated as heroes when they came back to Spain. Most had made enormous fortunes for themselves overseas. But Cortès himself died forgotten after quarrelling with Charles V, King of Spain.

The Venetians sent envoys to the courts of many sultans and princes. Unlike the Spanish, they prided themselves on their courtesy, and their understanding of the respect due to these great rulers and their ceremonial courts.

The Portuguese quickly established themselves as the most important merchants in the Far East, and in 1542 they became the first Europeans to visit Japan. This was the first ever contact between Japan and the West. They traded firearms for Japanese silk and spices. A few years later, the great Catholic missionary, Francis Xavier, settled in Japan and set up a successful mission there. But the Portuguese never tried to make Japan part of their empire, or subdue them; they were content with their profitable trading contacts.

# Travelling by Road

**Roads were vital to the life of the country; and yet they were often so bad that, in the winter, it was impossible to use them.** Heavy goods were often taken by river and sea, but even so there was plenty of traffic – farmers taking their produce to market, merchants and businessmen, and long-distance trade in light luxury items. The roads were usually made only of mud; and if there was very heavy traffic – if an army passed by for example, or the monarch with his great caravan of courtiers and furnishings – then the road could be ruined for months.

Each town or village was supposed to look after its roads and bridges; but many ignored this duty. Sometimes a holy man or hermit lived by the bridge and was made responsible for attending it. In Elizabeth's reign, the local knight or justice of the peace had to see that the roads were kept in good order. But it was an impossible task: builders sometimes even treated the roads as quarries and suddenly dug large holes for the stone or clay.

Even so, a lot of traffic did go by road for long distances. A man could ride sixty kilometres a day in comfort, and many goods were taken by road from, for instance, the Midlands to market in London, 160 kilometres or more away. Cattle might travel even further than this; special roads called drove roads ran for thousands of kilometres across Europe. It was common for cattle from Wales or Scotland to be driven down to London by these wide, grassy roads, travelling only a few kilometres a day to make sure they were still fat enough for market.

Because the roads were not good, people only travelled if they needed to. Usually, the point of a journey was to reach a new marketplace; each town was a focus of trade, both local and from far away. And so, because few people travelled for pleasure and many never went beyond their local market town all their lives, each town developed its own local customs and local pride. To go from one county town to the next could seem like a trip to a foreign country. The kings had to unite all these regions into a single unified nation.

A far greater number of people could read by 1600 than ever before, but shopkeepers still displayed pictorial signs to indicate their trade. There were more and more permanent shops in every town, taking the place of open market stalls.

The merchants of the Netherlands were amongst the richest in Europe; and they created their own style of furnishing and home decoration. Many paintings of this period show these sober people interested in the details of daily life rather than grand schemes of empire or affluence.

Most journeys took many days or even weeks, and the transport system of Europe needed a large number of inns. These could be found on every main road and in every town. On the passes of the Alps, in particular, there were huge inns. At such places, the tired traveller could always find good food,

cheery company, and a great deal to drink. Inns played an important part in life in 16th-century England providing places where friends could meet over a few drinks. After hops were introduced in Henry VIII's reign, beer drinking became very popular.

Pedlars travelled all round England and the continent, with a wide variety of goods. They sold their wares at markets and festivals, and tried to gain admission to the great houses to sell their cheap jewels and ribbons. Their little mirrors were extremely popular.

The corporations of the towns took on a new importance as the towns became richer. To express their pride in their town, they organized solemn processions on festival days. These festivals often were also religious occasions: 'miracle' plays were performed in the town square.

# Violence and Sudden Death

**Europe was becoming wealthier but violence and disease were just as common as in the Middle Ages.** Even in England, which was relatively peaceful, death from starvation, the plague, smallpox, in war or in a sudden brawl in the towns was a common event everywhere.

Civil wars racked most of Europe: France after 1572; the Holy Roman Empire from 1525 to 1555; the Netherlands from 1568; and in Italy there were continual wars until 1559, with armies causing distress wherever they went. Even worse, in the part of Europe close to the Mediterranean, there was a constant threat of the Barbary pirates who would come from the coast of North Africa and sack the towns and carry off the children to be sold as slaves in the East. Sometimes these children ended up in the households of great merchants of Lisbon or Venice; but they never saw their homes again.

As the population of Europe grew, more and more people went to the towns in search of work.

The towns soon became overcrowded, the jobs were taken and the authorities could not cope with the task of looking after all the beggars. Their numbers were never constant; after a couple of bad harvests, all the reserves of food would soon be used up, and thousands might leave home and die of starvation unless they could find charity.

Many people realized that the rich were getting richer while the numbers of poor were growing. The old ideas that kept the lower classes in their place broke down, and violent revolts occurred in the great towns of France and throughout the countryside of the Holy Roman Empire.

Even if they escaped this kind of violence, people were not safe. The plague, which had been the cause of the Black Death in the 1340s, revisited many cities, and no-one knew how to stop or predict its spread; after 1485 a new illness, smallpox, reached England to add yet another hazard to life in the towns. Small wonder that most wealthy men built their great houses in the countryside.

People who caught the plague almost always died within three days. No-one realized that the disease was spread by fleas carried on rats; all they could do was isolate the ill people. Dead and dying were thrown into mass graves together.

Groups of apprentices, sailors or students often went out together in the towns in search of a brawl. It was perhaps a way of working off the tension they felt about their overcrowded conditions, and the fact that they were very poor.

Armies were growing bigger and were infamous for the destruction they caused; food was requisitioned and anyone who argued might have his house burnt down and belongings taken. An army of Charles V even sacked Rome in 1527 and took the Pope prisoner.

The townspeople of Elizabethan England were terrified of the hordes of beggars who travelled from town to town. A law of 1601 said the poor were to be flogged (even if there were no jobs for them to do), although the crippled ones were given charity.

In England there were several local revolts in which unhappiness about rising prices was combined with dislike of the Protestant Reformation; the Cornishmen for instance, rebelled against the new Prayer Book in English in 1549. Usually these revolts were directed against the national govern-ment, and the local lords often supported the rebels. In the Peasants' War in Germany, however, in 1525, the peasants directly attacked their landlords. Such revolts were always put down very harshly, with the ringleaders and many of their followers executed.

# Life in the Country

**Life in the country was hard.** People worked from dawn till dusk to grow enough food; and they always depended on the harvest. If the crop failed for two years running, they had to kill their cows or pigs, and still they probably starved. For many peasants, life was becoming even harder – at least in the Middle Ages there were large commons on which everyone was allowed to graze their animals; now these commons were being seized by the landlords and fenced in to make sheep runs. As the price of food and other services went up, so the landlords tried to put up the rents of the peasants – or to force them out to put new tenants in.

English agriculture was changing in the 16th century. The old feudal manors had broken up, and instead there were a large number of well-to-do yeoman farmers, who had medium-sized, compact estates; and there were also many tenant farmers who had to pay rents, but no other dues, to their lords. In the 1530s, the biggest change of all occurred – Henry VIII seized all the lands belonging to the monasteries, and much of that of the bishoprics. He then sold most of it to his friends, or to local noblemen or yeomen, whoever would pay the best price. As a result, many people found themselves with new landlords after 1540, and often they complained that these new men were interested only in taking the profit from their estates, and did not care about the land or their tenants. Perhaps this was true, and perhaps not, but the Elizabethan age saw both a large number of fine, solid new farmhouses built all over England – a sure sign of prosperity for some – and also many people driven to the towns in search of jobs.

Even so, the English farmers prided themselves on being freer, and much better off, than their counterparts on the continent. In Spain, for instance, there was a huge flock of sheep that was allowed to wander all over the country, and no-one was allowed to hinder its movements or keep it off his land. In much of eastern Europe, the peasants were still serfs, and were not even allowed to leave their estates or own any property. They had to work very hard, and, sometimes, there would be rebellions. These usually failed and severe punishment would follow.

In England there were two distinct agricultural regions. In the south and midlands, there was the wealthy 'champion' country, where wheat and other crops were grown; in the west and north there was much poorer soil and smaller farms, where farmers concentrated on livestock.

Despite their hard work, there were many festivals in the country. People would celebrate the harvest, Midsummer's Day, or Mayday. Many of these festivals recalled ancient rites intended to ensure that the earth would stay fertile. They were a time for dancing and romancing.

New animals were introduced to Europe's farms by explorers. The turkey was a native of Mexico, and was brought back to Europe by the Spaniards in the 1520s. Guinea fowl were brought back from Africa by the Portuguese. Both were a welcome source of food.

New crops became common in Europe – the potato and sweetcorn were brought from America where they were the regular food of the Indians. Cauliflowers, melons and artichokes were plants which the Arabs took to Spain in the Middle Ages, and now flourished everywhere.

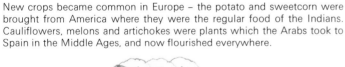

Townsmen often bought the old estates of the nobility or the Church. They farmed them more efficiently than before, growing more food to meet the demand of the large towns. In England, the Cecil family, for example, rose to prominence, and became men of importance for centuries.

# Mining

**In the 16th century, mining for metals and for coal suddenly became a flourishing industry all over Europe.** It was the first sign of the enormous expansion in production that, two hundred years later, would be known as the Industrial Revolution. The main centres for mining were in central Europe. There had been silver mines for centuries in Germany, but now coal and iron mining became big business there too. The Fuggers, who were the greatest bankers in 16th-century Europe, founded their fortune on iron and silver mines in Germany; a German, Georgius Agricola, was the first man to write a book on the techniques of mining, and Queen Elizabeth imported a number of German miners to England.

In the Middle Ages, coal was hardly mined at all; wood or charcoal was used for heating houses. But now most of the coal-bearing regions of England were discovered and many rich land-owners used coal as their main fuel on their great estates. Newcastle began to grow rich on selling coal to London, and a little coal was even exported overseas.

Other mines were flourishing in England too. In Cornwall and Devon, the tin mines that the Romans had known were still prosperous. Like coal, it was still possible for anyone with a shovel to dig tin from the soil, but soon both industries came into the hands of wealthy landlords or traders, who could afford to grade and distribute the product. The English lead industry, too, was one of the most important in Europe. It was based in the Mendip hills, in Cumberland and in the Peak District. There was so much building work being done that this industry enjoyed a period of huge prosperity until the 1540s.

This was the beginning of the great period of England's industries. A few of the mines were well organized, and employed a large number of people. New kinds of water pumps were used although there were no steam engines yet to pump out deep mines. But most of the work was still done by hand.

There were rich silver mines at Kutna Hora, in Bohemia, where new ideas made mining more efficient. The mines were very deep and narrow and the miners had to wear white costumes because it was so dark; but conditions were far better than at the terrible mines of South America such as Potosí.

At Kutna Hora the stones were loaded onto waggons which ran along wooden rails to make them easier to handle; and then they were loaded into buckets and hauled to the surface by means of a system of pulleys and the silver was then extracted from the ore.

Belgium had many coal mines, which supplied the forges of the valley of the river Meuse. Horses were tied to a windlass, which pulled up the baskets of coal. This was slow; but it meant that deep mines could be used.

In England, in the 1550s, most of the coal mining was still done in shallow mines. The coal was mainly used by blacksmiths close by or to heat people's houses. In the next 50 years, much larger mines were dug.

Deep mines are often flooded, and sometimes a pump was installed, driven by a huge water wheel on the surface. It used the principle of the village pump to bring up the water from below, in a number of small steps.

A large number of people worked in mines. The minerals were dug out of the rock by simple hand tools. It was an exhausting job, and a dangerous one. The roof might cave in, and explosions were common.

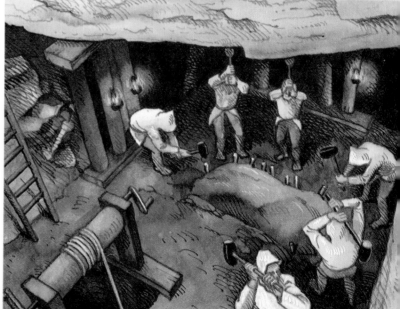

# Metalworking

**As armies grew larger and larger, and a limitless demand for firearms and cannons developed, the metal working industry developed new techniques that had great importance for the future.** In about 1500 the blast furnace, a method of extracting the pure metal from iron ore dug out of the ground, was developed in the region around Liège, in the Low Countries. This invention meant that the quality of the metal could be improved, and large objects could now be 'cast' in molten iron, instead of beaten into shape. They were therefore much stronger than before, and much cheaper to make.

Metal working, on a small scale, had been an ancient skill practised wherever the ores could be mined. In England, there were ancient metal working centres in the Midlands, in Cornwall and in the Weald of Sussex and Kent. By 1500 Birmingham and Sheffield were already known for their knives and nails; and during the 16th century, their industry improved as coal could be used to make the furnaces much hotter. At the same time, the Weald became a centre of heavy metal work. In the 1540s, Henry VIII at last realized the need for modern artillery for his armies and introduced German experts to set up the first blast furnaces and cannon foundries. Cast-iron cannons were far better and safer than the old, hand-beaten ones. By 1600 these foundries, now mainly run by Frenchmen, were producing about 100 tonnes of iron a year. The industry needed a great deal of machinery and investment, and so it was organized into large factories. Even so, the fuel for the furnaces was still charcoal and wood – the iron works cleared the Weald area of much of its forest.

As well as iron working, copper and silver works flourished, especially in Germany and Bohemia. In Sweden, too, the metal industry became the basis of the country's future wealth. But Europe's main metalworking centre was in the Low Countries, adding to the already high concentration of industry in that area.

Delicate metalwork flourished at this time, especially with the silversmiths who produced finely decorated dinner services for the great households. Iron, too, was now used for more and more everyday goods.

The first blast furnaces were fuelled by wood or charcoal, but in the region of Liège coal and even oil were used. The molten metal flowed out of the furnace and was cooled in ponds. New methods of improving the system were constantly being found.

Huge bellows, driven by a water-wheel, was one method used to make furnaces hot enough to refine ore. Water-wheels also drove the hammers in forges. In the Weald, special 'hammer-ponds' were built to keep enough water to run these wheels.

Furnaces similar to those used for ironworking were installed in the glass factories of Venice. Glass window panes were made by putting molten glass on the end of a rod and spinning it very quickly as it solidified. The force of the spinning made the glass into a flat circle. It was then cooled in a bed of sand. The techniques of glass making were thought to be a valuable secret by the Venetians, who issued dire threats against any of their crafts-men who went to work in other places. Even so, their skills were known all over Europe by the 1570s.

# Crafts and Industries

These were the days of the first factories: workshops where a number of labourers might work for a daily wage, and have no hope of becoming their own masters. In metal-working, printing and weaving, a successful trades-man might expand his business and take on employees, to be able to make more and cheaper goods than he could manage by the old-fashioned system of apprentices.

These factories were often hard places to work: sometimes, the town council would try to regulate hours and make sure that all the workers had a good rest at lunchtime, but even so, many people worked twelve or fourteen hours a day. Employees could be dismissed at a moment's notice, and their wages could be cut. The first strikes occurred in France and Italy in the 17th century.

But it was not all hard work. There were many religious holidays, and much work was stopped by the winter, so that it was rare to work more than three days a week, on average; and there were no machines to force people to work quickly when they were tired. Most industries were still organized in the old way, with a few craftsmen, who took on young boys as apprentices to do the dirty work and learn the skills of the trade for seven years. These apprentices usually lived with their masters, and were often well treated by them. This was a period of great craftsmanship, when magnificent armour, furniture, and guns were made; many craftsmen worked for a particular member of the nobility, or for the royal court. The craftsman could usually decorate the piece as he wished, and the decorations of the 16th century display great skill and imagination.

In towns there would be a wide range of industries and crafts – perhaps twenty or thirty, ranging from making armour to candles. In the villages, there were far fewer, and many of the craftsmen would work in the fields for half the time, and only practise their skills when a particular job was needed.

In Italy there were craftsmen who were considered the equal of the great painters. The glass factories of Murano, an island in Venice, were famous for their vases and decorative pieces; and the goldsmiths of Florence, who worked in tiny shops right under the noses of the passers-by, inspired many painters. The famous sculptor, Benvenuto Cellini, was originally trained as a goldsmith. More and more great houses had a collection of 'plate': one of the most popular pieces was a huge centrepiece for the table known as the 'standing salt', made of gold, silver or crystal.

Italy was the home of fine cloth, and Italians visited China to find out the secrets of silk-making. But Europe's best silk industry was based at Lyons, in France. In this picture, cocoons are being soaked and the thread unwound.

Woodworking was a vital industry, since all buildings and ships were mainly made of wood. England was famous for the quality of its oak and its beech. As furniture came more into demand, there grew up more and more fine work for carpenters.

The Netherlands was the home of the glass-grinding industry. New skills in grinding and polishing glass were developed to make spectacles much cheaper and better than before. The Dutch also made the lenses used in early telescopes.

Weaving was much the most important English industry in 1500; English cloth was sold to Flanders. After 1550, this market collapsed, and other industries took over. Other famous weaving centres were Milan, Florence, Genoa and Venice; their cloth was popular all over Europe.

# Printing

**Johannes Gutenberg, a German who worked in Strasburg, produced the first printed books in Europe in the 1450s.** His invention led to great changes in the history of Europe, bringing many new ideas and new information to people for the first time.

The business of printing was slow and complicated. Each letter had to be cast or moulded in metal and arranged in a tray in the right position. The tray was put in the bottom of the press, and covered in ink; paper was put on top, and pressed down by means of a lever on a screw. But, however complicated the process, it was quicker than copying books by hand. By the end of the 16th century, an expert printer could produce 3,000 copies of a page in a day – a rate of one every 15 seconds.

The new techniques soon spread to every city of Europe. Most printers were lone craftsmen, working perhaps with an apprentice. In the early days, they were well-educated men who had to decide what to print as well as doing all the work themselves. Often they were associated with the new ideas of the Renaissance, or with the reformers of the Church. As the demand for books grew, some printers built up factories with up to 100 employees.

The books of the 15th century were almost as beautiful as hand-written books. Gradually the printers developed designs for letters that were easy to read and did not imitate the longhand Gothic script. The subjects of the books varied a lot; as well as religious works, they included new editions of Greek and Roman writers; manuals on mining, agriculture and science; public notices, newspapers, broadsheets and ballad sheets which told the news in the form of a song; and even advertisements for shop-keepers. For the first time, the written word reached almost everyone.

The developments in printing meant that knowledge was now made available to many more people, and no longer limited to the clergy. School books and Bibles were printed in large quantities, and many schools were set up. Foreign works were translated, and scholars argued about these theories and put forward new ideas of their own. Many people, however, were still illiterate.

There were a lot of different aspects to the trade of an early printer. As well as actually printing the pages, he also had to make his own letters in metal. Here a printer pours molten metal, mixed tin and lead, into a letter mould to form the letters he requires.

Printing led to a sudden demand for paper, and in some places mechanical mills were built. Here, river water drove an axle to turn beaters which turned hemp and flax into pulp. This pulp was then refined, pressed and dried in sheets, to become paper.

Most printers sold their own works direct to the public. Books were still not cheap, and were usually bound in leather and finely finished; many were made only at the request of a particular patron. Printing was introduced to England early, in 1476, by William Caxton; but it was not very successful at first – there were only four presses in the whole country by 1500. Caxton was a very skilful printer, and translated many of his books himself from Latin, French and Dutch. He also designed his own typefaces and added woodcuts to illustrate the texts.

Many books, especially handbooks on science or medicine, had illustrations in them. These were usually done by woodcuts. The artist cut away the background of the picture from a flat piece of wood or leather, which was then inked and pressed between two cylinders.

Pedlars sometimes had printed advertisements telling people of the town at which they had just arrived of their wares. Only a few villagers could read, and these people told the others what the notices said. In this way, everyone could learn all the news.

# Children

**A child's life in the 16th century was a hard one.** Children were set to work at an early age; they had to be respectful to all adults, as even their parents treated them as lower than the servants; and they were beaten for every little mistake. They had a lot of games to play, and toys to play with; but children suffered badly from illnesses – about one in every three or four died before the age of ten.

Unlike the Middle Ages, this was an age of education. Members of the upper classes had private tutors, and were taught languages from an early age; Queen Elizabeth could speak Latin and Greek fluently at the age of nine. There were many schools founded in England, especially after the Dissolution of the Monasteries – before that the monks had been the most important teachers in the country. Now, grammar schools were set up in almost every small town for the children of local tradesmen. The boys and sometimes, though less frequently, the girls of the town were sent to these schools to learn to read and write. Mostly they learned about the Bible, and about the Romans and Greeks. These schools were run by one or two schoolmasters and their wives. They had very little equipment other than desks and a few books.

Boys who were not sent to school might be apprenticed to a local craftsman. Before the age of ten, these apprentices were sent away from home to live in the house of the master craftsman for seven years or more to learn his trade and act as his servant. Other children were sent out to work in the fields at the age of four or five, at first to mind the sheep or pigs, and later to do more strenuous jobs. The girls had to help with the cooking and washing.

Children were not allowed very much time to enjoy growing up. They were dressed in adult clothes, and given adult jobs. But, in compensation, when they grew up they would spend a lot of their time playing like children.

Many schools that are now large, rich and famous were founded in the 16th century. Some were set up for the children of local tradesmen; and others were boarding schools for people living all over the country. Similar schools were set up all over Europe, especially in the Protestant countries. Many children stayed at school from seven to fifteen, and had only four or five weeks holiday each year. Teachers believed that it was best to beat the child for every mistake that he made – in that way they hoped that the pupil would take extra care and so would learn his lessons quickly.

Some boys became apprentices to artists, just as in any other trade. At first they would just mix the paints. After a year or two, the master gave a few drawing lessons, and eventually allowed the pupil to paint the background of the pictures.

In Catholic countries, most of the teaching was still done by monks. The children wore monastic costumes and the lessons were mainly on reading the Bible. Both Protestants and Catholics considered religious and moral education as important as reading, writing and arithmetic.

Students at university were often thought to be rowdy and drunken – people complained that they did not care about their studies at all. At Heidelberg, one of the most famous universities, the students used to keep the towns-people awake by singing and ringing bells.

Schoolmasters were fond of beating their children. To make it even more painful, they used bundles of birch twigs tied together. But the children were used to such treatment – they usually got the same punishment at home as well.

# Girls and Women

**Men treated women as pieces of property to be bought and sold in marriage.** If a man had a daughter, he taught her enough to be a good housewife, then, perhaps when she was still only seven years old, chose a fiancé for her, a man who would be a good social match. She might be married at thirteen, with her husband many years older. He would treat her almost as a servant; he would check her accounts and criticize her housekeeping while she served up his meals or stood respectfully behind him and accepted what he said. He could beat her if he liked – she had no rights at law against her husband. She often had to run her husband's business. It was the same for both the rich and the poor; and the wives of farmers were expected to help in the fields, as well as do all the housework.

Things were only beginning to improve for the wives of townsmen, the merchants of London, Florence or the Netherlands. These men treated their wives as partners in business; and the growing amount of time and money they spent on decorating their homes showed the growing importance they placed on domestic life and on women. In Florence in the 1490s, women made clear how much they wanted their place in society to change – they supported the revolutionary monk Savonarola in his attempt to clear the city of all luxuries and vices. They even threw their jewellery and fine clothes on his great fires.

In some ways the position of women improved by 1600. There were several important queens in Europe, women such as Elizabeth, who proved herself to be just as good at ruling a country as any man. Eighty years earlier, Henry VIII had such little regard for women that he married six times to make sure that he had a son; he threw his wives aside when he lost interest in them or, as in the case of Catherine of Aragon, when they were past child-bearing age. Things had improved at Elizabeth's court, when every courtier was expected to be as gallant to women as Walter Raleigh, who laid down his coat so that Elizabeth could avoid a puddle!

The women of Venice used to bleach their hair in the sun. They put on a large straw hat without a crown to protect their complexions from being tanned, because sun tans were thought to be a sign of a low position in society.

Well-to-do women had little work to do, and enjoyed spinning and embroidering. Mary, Queen of Scots helped to set the fashion for embroidery when she was kept prisoner by Elizabeth. One of her guardians, Bess of Hardwick, worked on her tapestries with her.

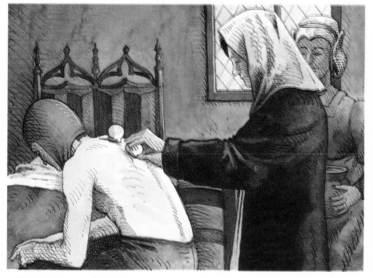

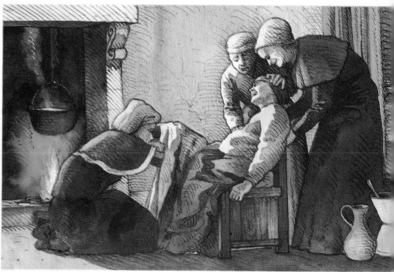

Some nuns worked as nurses for the poor in England, at least until the 1530s when the convents and monasteries were suppressed. Many people suffered from complaints of their lungs, and to reduce the blood pressure, heated glass cups were applied to the patient's skin.

In Holland, a woman about to have a baby kept her dress on all the time. Only the midwife and the women of the family were allowed to attend her. Many women and children died in childbirth, but large families were common.

The royal courts gave women an increasingly important place. They were expected to be skilled in the arts such as music, dancing and literature, and even science; Queen Elizabeth, for instance, could speak Latin and Greek when she was a child. Courtiers wrote poems to the women, and hoped to entrance them with their fine words and the richness of their ideas. There were many songs, known as madrigals, written for men and women to sing together, on themes like love and happiness; not religious songs like most earlier music.

# Religion

**In the 16th century, everyone believed in God.** Everyone believed in the Devil, too. Religion was an essential and basic part of life, and going to heaven or hell was a vital question to all.

Religion affected everything that most people did. Desperately dependent on a good harvest, they prayed to God for fine weather; terrified of the Plague and thinking that it was a scourge from God, they whipped themselves to atone for their sins. If a family suffered bad luck, if the children died or the hayrick burned down, it was said to be the work of the Devil. Many women, young and old, were burned to death because people thought they were witches, servants of the Devil who worked charms to curse people they hated.

For most people, the Church meant regular services which were conducted in Latin. They were reassuring even if the congregation could not understand a word that was said; it meant the village priest – who acted as friend, adviser and even doctor in many villages and to whom everyone had to pay a tenth of their yearly produce; it meant the local great monastery or cathedral – a fine local building, a school for many children and the centre of a great estate. Some people resented the Church, but many were upset when things began to change – when the monasteries disappeared in England, the people of the north rebelled; and when services in English were brought in by Edward VI, the people of Cornwall also took to arms.

To the powerful and the educated, the question of the Church was different. Scholars argued about the details of the central mysteries of Christianity; but everyone agreed that religion was the best way of making the country contented and united. In Spain, in 1478, the Spanish Inquisition was founded to find heretics; in England, Henry VIII declared himself Supreme Governer of the Church. In The Holy Roman Empire, princes were said in 1555 to have the power to decide whether their subjects ought to be Protestant or Catholic. Religion was a vital part of the fabric of society, and people whose religious views differed from the accepted ones were often persecuted.

The pope behaved more like a great prince, the equal or better of the kings, than a spiritual leader. Several popes proved themselves on the battle field, fighting to protect the papal lands in Italy. But after 1540, popes became more spiritual.

A child's religious life began at baptism. If a child died before he was baptized, it was thought that he could never go to heaven. But some reformers said that only adults should be baptized. These reformers were thought to be dangerous men.

Explorers in Africa, Asia and the Americas took Christianity with them. They claimed that it was their duty to show the truth to the native heathens who would otherwise go to hell. Very often, the missionaries paid no attention to the religions already flourishing amongst the natives; some-times the natives had to choose between baptism and execution. But in many parts, the missionaries did good work. They improved the worst conditions of the Peruvians in the silver mines, and they became popular and successful in India and Japan.

If a house seemed to be taken over by the Devil or if people thought that a witch had cast a spell on it, the priest would carry out the ceremony of exorcism. Using holy water, his crucifix, and a holy candle, he drove the Devil away.

People were always buried, although in some parts of France they were not put in coffins. Heretics, though, were not buried; they were burned to death, and their heart might be thrown into the river. This, like other executions, was always done in public.

# Christians in Conflict

**The Church had for centuries been plagued by ignorant priests, worldly monks, powerful bishops, and lazy popes.** It was felt that the Church had been preying on the faith of the people, and using their trust to become rich and powerful. In 1517, when a preacher toured the Rhineland selling indulgences, a monk, Martin Luther, attacked this example of the Church's greed. He eventually found himself criticizing the authority of the Pope and other basic Catholic beliefs. Luther declared that a priest should be the servant of the community in which he worked; that services should be in the everyday language so that everyone could understand them. Above all, he argued that a simple faith was enough to win someone a place in heaven. The Catholics angrily opposed him. They based their arguments on the authority of Church Councils: Luther appealed to the Bible.

Whatever the rights and wrongs of the arguments, this dispute was eagerly taken up by opponents of the Church's power. Henry VIII, who wanted to make the Church subject to his own authority, used it as an excuse to declare himself, and not the Pope, head of the English Church; many princes in the Holy Roman Empire saw in it a chance to become free of the power of the Catholic Emperor.

All over Europe, arguments raged, taken over by political forces that were far removed from the religious ideas from which they arose. The Catholics staged a counterattack: Queen Mary tried to re-impose Catholicism in England, burning as heretics many Protestants, including the Archbishop of Canterbury, Thomas Cranmer; and her husband, Philip II of Spain, allowed the Spanish Inquisition to burn anyone who was religiously unorthodox. He also fought a lifelong war to oppose Protestantism in the Netherlands, and even launched the Spanish Armada to rescue England from the Protestant Queen Elizabeth. France, too, was torn by religious strife for 30 years. A strict Protestant sect ruled over Geneva.

The reformers met at first in private houses, but eventually managed to build churches in the style that they preferred. Whereas the Catholic churches were dark and covered in rich decorations, and the priest and altar were cut off from the rest of the congregation, the reformed churches were bare and white. The Protestants loved sermons, and many preachers would go on for two hours or more. They told the people how to behave, and even spoke on political matters. Their services were always given in the language of the congregation.

Henry VIII closed all the monasteries in England, and took their lands, in the 1530s. The monks had to make do as best they could. The monasteries had played an important part in nursing the sick, teaching the young and looking after the poor.

In many places the Protestants destroyed the statues and stained glass that adorned the churches. They considered that decorated churches distracted people from thinking about God. In England, most of the monasteries were pulled down after they had been closed; their stone, lead and timber were

Protestants and Catholics were both prepared to kill those who opposed them; the wars of religion in France and Germany were long-drawn out, bitter and very bloody. Queen Mary of England killed about 250 Protestants in her five-year reign, and exiled many others.

used for repairing other buildings, and in particular for building the new country houses of the men who had bought up the old monastery estates. Few monastic buildings still survive intact, except for those attached to cathedrals, or those turned into schools.

# Illness and Doctors

**If a person became ill, he had far less chance of recovering than he would have today.** He had a choice, depending on his station in life, of going to a physician, a surgeon or a herbalist. The physician was a man learned in the classics and philosophy, and his diagnoses were based on the study of the patient's urine. The surgeon might be the dentist and barber too; he had little real knowledge of what he was doing, or of the problems of infection. Surgeons often used clumsy tools, and the patient had no anaesthetic to save him from the pain. The herbalist, on the other hand, might apply all sorts of concoctions made from plants or infusions of strange parts of animals, such as worms' livers or newts' tongues. Some of these substances had real medicinal value but most of them were dreamed up either out of ignorance or to cheat the patient.

It was generally thought that the body was made up of the four basic elements – earth, air, fire and water – and that medicine should attempt to restore the normal balance between these four. For many diseases, the only known remedy was to reduce the blood pressure; this was done by applying leeches to the patient to suck out his blood. Considering all this, it is perhaps surprising that people lived as long as they did.

Gradually, though, medical knowledge improved. Firstly, the surgeons who worked for the great armies began to find better ways of treating wounds. The famous French surgeon, Ambroise Paré, learned that red-hot irons should not be applied to bullet wounds, and found ways of tying the arteries when a limb had to be amputated. Doctors, such as the German Paracelsus, attacked the ancient Greek theories which the physicians still followed. People began to study how the human body actually works. Dissecting corpses was generally forbidden, and so the anatomist Vesalius had to be brave enough to steal dead bodies from the public gallows, in the middle of the night.

Many plants were known to be good medicines: deadly nightshade was thought (correctly, in small quantities) to be good for the heart, and cherry stalks for the kidneys. Many old women collected herbs for their livelihood; they were sometimes known as white witches.

Doctors who tried to find new methods of treating the sick were sometimes accused of witchcraft – seeking the Devil's help in their studies. Perhaps some doctors actually did do this; Paracelsus, for instance, tried to base his medical theories on mystical and magical ideas.

In the Middle Ages there had been a very few public dissections of the bodies of criminals, carried out by physicians who pointed out the various organs of the body to anyone who wished to learn. But they made no attempt to find out how the body actually worked. Vesalius was the first

Military surgeons were the most skilled of their profession; and the use of guns made their task much harder. By the late 16th century, some military surgeons were performing successful operations on their patients. Few surgeons in England were skilled enough to do this.

man to make accurate observations of the body by dissection, and in 1543 he published a book that brought a completely new understanding of the human body. Public dissections then became more common; the corpses were still usually of criminals.

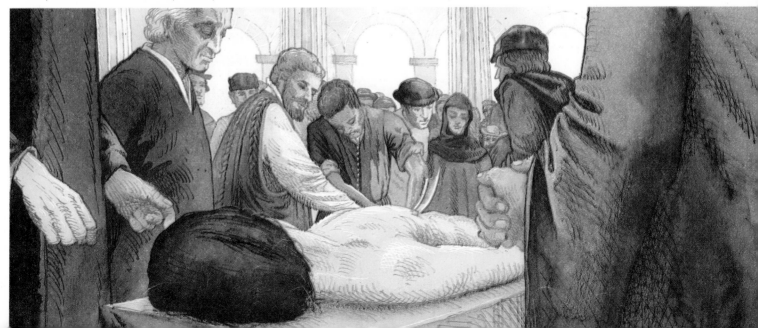

# The 'New Learning'

During the 15th century, scholars and scientists won greater and greater importance in Europe. Kings listened to what they had to say, and the Church saw they could pose a grave threat to traditional teaching. Why did scholars become so influential at this time?

A movement, known as the 'New Learning', began in Italy with the study of the ancient Greek and Roman authors. This led to a revival of the spirit of inquiry that characterized the ancient Greeks. Men were no longer content to accept authority: they began to think for themselves and to ask reasons and proof of what they were told to believe. The 'New Learning' was at first confined to a small group of scholars, who knew each other personally; but after the invention of printing, it became far more widespread. Amongst its most important scholars were the Fleming Erasmus, and his English friends Thomas More and John Colet. In Italy, the best known is Niccolo Machiavelli. He questioned all the principles on which rulers based their authority.

The daring of Machiavelli, and of Erasmus who criticized the abuses of the Church, meant that these men were seen as a danger to the old order. The Catholic Church set up the 'Index' of prohibited books; it read every new book, and banned all those which it did not like. But even so, the new ideas spread: the Catholics could not stop Protestants printing their books, and ideas also got around by word of mouth, and even in song. Similarly, the work of the scientists was seen by the Church as a grave threat. Men like Galileo and Copernicus were questioning the Church's teaching that the earth was the centre of the universe. They began to collect evidence that the earth moved round the sun. The Church thought that man was at the centre of all creation, and so the universe must revolve around the earth.

Perhaps the reason for the importance of the scholars of the 'New Learning' was that their work implied a new idea, an idea that attacked the whole basis of the medieval Church. This idea was that men should be able to think for themselves, and that each individual had the right to his own opinions – the antithesis of medieval religious teaching.

Leonardo da Vinci, the famous painter, was also a highly original scientist who designed all sorts of machines. Using newly-found principles of physics, he designed flying machines, submarines, tanks and guns. He was many centuries ahead of his time.

Libraries were built in many towns, where students could find a large number of new books. As more and more people could now read, it was possible for people to educate themselves; the Church could not keep up its old monopoly of knowledge.

Scientists had to build and keep up their own workshops and laboratories; not many could afford such spacious conditions as these. The universities rarely provided any assistance, and princes only gave scientists patronage if they were working on explosives, or military machines. This picture shows

the laboratory of a chemist or alchemist who used furnaces and presses to try and turn iron or copper into gold. Even in an age of the new sciences – astronomy and physics – the ancient practice of alchemy was still carried on by many people.

Kings and princes liked to surround themselves with students of the 'New Learning'. Thomas More, for instance, became Chancellor to Henry VIII, Thomas Wolsey founded a college at Oxford, and the scholar Roger Ascham was tutor to Henry's daughter Elizabeth.

Several leading scientists were persecuted by the Church, which was afraid of their influence. In 1600, Giordano Bruno was burnt as a heretic; soon after Galileo, too, was forced to renounce his theories of astronomy because of Church opposition.

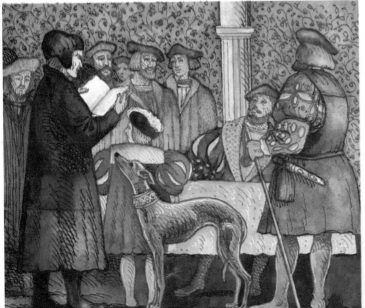

# Artists

**The years around 1500 were one of the greatest ever periods for art.** Men such as Michelangelo, Leonardo da Vinci and Raphael, are still thought to be amongst the greatest artists who ever lived. Some of their important works were on so huge a scale – the decoration of the entire ceiling of a church, or a whole palace – that they took years to complete. Suddenly everyone with money – kings, popes, merchants, noblemen – was interested in spending it on paintings. In the Middle Ages artists had worked anonymously, like craftsmen who never tried to develop a style of their own; but now the names of the artists were known all over Europe, and each one tried to create a style that expressed his own personal vision.

This great change in art is known as the Renaissance; it began in Italy, especially in Florence and Rome. In these places the artists competed to devise more skilful pictures, a better system of perspective (the illusion of three dimensions on a flat surface) and better methods of colouring. Their pictures seemed to show man as more confident, more glorious and more beautiful than ever before. In this, the artists were echoing the ideas of the new scholars, and the confidence of the wealthy merchants.

Gradually, the new ideas spread to the rest of Europe. Early in the 15th century, Albrecht Dürer took them to Germany, and from there Hans Holbein introduced them to England. Holbein worked as court portrait-painter to Henry VIII, and was even sent off to paint a faithful likeness of the women whom Henry thought he might wish to marry. But the art of the great Renaissance painters did not become really popular in England until the 17th century; neither Henry nor Elizabeth made a conscious attempt to encourage its success. By contrast, Francis I of France invited Leonardo da Vinci to work for him, and then brought a group of Italian artists to decorate his new palace at Fontainebleu. In doing so he completely changed artistic style in France.

Decorating the walls of an enormous church was a huge undertaking, and one man could not do it on his own. Most artists ran workshops, with teams of apprentices and assistants to help them. The technique which was usually used to decorate large walls was known as fresco; the wall was first plastered, and the painting done on the plaster while it was still wet. It was essential to dry the wall off very quickly after it had been painted, and so burning cauldrons were put under the newly painted areas.

A boy who wanted to become an artist had to be apprenticed to a master, just as for any other trade. He would spend several years mixing the paints, cleaning the brushes or even lifting the master up to the area he was working on.

Michelangelo, who was a great sculptor as well as a painter, chose his huge blocks of marble from a quarry at Carrara, in central Italy. Painting and sculpture were both expensive occupations – no-one worked without a patron to pay the bills.

Many statues were made in bronze. The artist made a wax model; he then covered it with a plaster mould. When heat was applied, the wax melted and molten bronze was poured in. The mould was then cut away, leaving the finished sculpture.

# The Glory of the Monarchy

In the days of the Crusades, Europe had been thought of as Christendom – a single society of Christians, ruled over by the Pope. It was now, by contrast, a collection of separate countries. In each of these countries, the monarch was seen as the embodiment of the nation: the glory of his court enshrined the glory of his entire people. As so the kings of the 16th century – men like Henry VIII and Francis I of France – created huge, splendid courts; they fought wars for no other reason than to show off their bravery and their warlike skills; they overawed their subjects by a combination of brute force and splendour. As an extreme demonstration of their belief in splendour, Henry VIII and Francis I met each other in 1520 at the Field of the Cloth of Gold in France, a diplomatic show in which their entire courts were housed for days in magnificent tents while jousts, feasts and pageants went on.

The monarchs claimed more and more power; and they developed a better and better administration to get it. For Henry VIII, his ministers Thomas Wolsey and Thomas Cromwell reorganized the administration; yet both of these men died in disgrace. Under Elizabeth, a minister's life was safer, but all acknowledged the Queen's supremacy; indeed, her whole court was so centred around her person that she was venerated almost as a god.

Unlike the Middle Ages, there were no nobles in England strong enough to threaten the monarch's position. And yet this power was already being challenged. In England, the Reformation which had brought so much power to the monarch, also gave Parliament, and especially the House of Commons, extra prestige. By the end of Elizabeth's reign, it was claiming the right to criticize the Queen's policies. In other countries, too, the rule of the monarchs was being questioned. Even in Spain, the Cortes was summoned to voice the grievances of the provinces, while Mary Queen of Scots had actually been driven from Scotland.

Venice was ruled over by a prince, known as the doge. To express the glory of Venice, the doge took part in some of the most magnificent ceremonies and processions ever organized. He wore a golden cloak, and his head-dress was inlaid with precious stones.

In the Netherlands, there was a revolt against the rule of the Spanish king, which brought independence to Holland. The new state was made up of townsmen and merchants; they became the first people to give up monarchy altogether, and swear allegiance to a republic instead.

The royal courts, and the king's wars, had to be paid for in taxes. In 1524, a taxation assessment was made in England even more detailed than the Domesday Book; and in the next 15 years, Cromwell reorganized the whole system of the civil service.

Queen Elizabeth went to Parliament to instruct its members of her wishes. She considered that Parliament should discuss how to carry them out, and should vote on new taxes; but not criticize her policies or advise her how to behave. But many members of the Commons did far more than this; they

tried to influence her religious policy, and even tell her to get married. Several MPs were sent to the Tower of London for speeches that displeased her; but by the time of her death, the Commons, which represented the country gentlemen and the merchants, was gaining the upper hand.

# The Art of War – I

**When Henry Tudor won the battle of Bosworth Field in 1485 to bring an end to the Wars of the Roses, England had a period of relative peace that lasted for well over 50 years.** The rest of Europe was not so lucky; in 1494 the French king, Charles VIII, claimed the dukedom of Milan, and thus began a war, fought mainly in Italy, that lasted until 1559, and involved most of the continental European powers as well as the Italian city states. To share in the glory, Henry VIII launched a number of expeditions to Europe, mainly against his arch-rival Francis I, but these were insignificant, and the English army was out-of-date and uninvolved with the latest developments in warfare.

War was not yet fought by large, national armies. The expeditions were launched by the king, who paid for them out of his own treasury, he did not always rely on his own people to fight for him if better soldiers could be found elsewhere. This was the heyday of the mercenaries, known as the condottieri; troops of Germans, Scots or Genoese were available to the highest bidder. Above all, the great mercenaries of the time were Swiss. The Swiss infantry were for a long time thought to be invincible; an opposing commander would try to buy them over to his own side, rather than do battle with them.

Yet the reign of the mercenaries and the small armies began to pass with the introduction of effective firearms. Gunpowder had been used in battle since the 14th century; but guns had been clumsy and hard to use and archers and cavalry were still more dangerous. But by 1500 the musket or 'arquebus' was brought in, the first truly useful small gun. It could shoot through even the thickest armour. The Spaniards were the first to use the arquebus, while the French relied more on artillery fire from big cannons. This artillery won the French a great victory at Marignano in 1515; but at Pavia, in 1525, the arquebus fire of the Hapsburg armies destroyed the French army.

Armies in the field needed a lot of support – food, clothing, military supplies, housing and medical assistance. Some of this was requisitioned from the nearby towns or farms, and the rest brought from home. Some armies, especially the mercenaries, tried to set up rules of behaviour towards the civilians – but extreme discipline was needed to maintain these rules. Thomas Wolsey established his authority in England by managing to supply Henry VIII's expeditions – often an extraordinary feat of organization when fighting across the Channel.

Heavily armoured knights still took part in battles. The English army had very few arquebusiers; even at the battle of Flodden, in 1513, when it won a great victory over the Scots, cavalry and archers were largely responsible for the success.

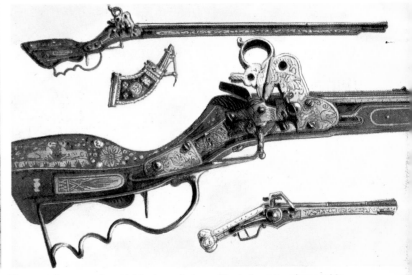

The arquebus was often highly decorated, an object of great craftsmanship. Early examples were ignited by a wick, but this was inefficient in the rain and the flintlock was soon developed. Pistols that could be fired from horseback were important in modernizing the cavalry.

Two armies face each other before a battle; apart from the nobility and knights, the armies mostly fought on foot, in tight ranks. Almost all the soldiers were experienced in battle – many hoped to make their livelihood out of warfare. Since the mercenary captains had to hire their men themselves, and relied on their reputation for future employment, they did their best to avoid battles that would lead to great bloodshed. As a result, the arquebus, which made battles much more murderous, brought the end of the domination of the mercenary armies in Europe.

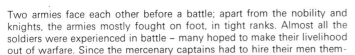

# The Art of War – II

**The art of war changed in the 16th century for two reasons.** Firstly because of the use of gunpowder, and secondly because strong, popular passions were being brought into play. Up until the 1520s, most wars had been fought in support of the dynastic or family disputes of the kings and princes – the ordinary soldiers had little interest in the war itself except perhaps as a means of getting rich. But in the wars of religion, the civil wars and the wars in which countries fought to save their national independence – such as the revolt of the Netherlands from Spanish rule, or the defence of England against the Spanish Armada – the ordinary soldier now felt he had something to fight for. And as the use of guns meant that larger and larger armies were needed, the face of war changed dramatically.

Several countries developed national armies. The most famous, and most feared, was the Spanish infantry, known as the *tiercos.* The king of France kept a standing army of 18,000 men – a huge number for that time; and even in England, which was only slightly affected by the wars of the period, a national militia was organized. According to this system, men of each county were instructed in the basics of warfare – the use of a musket and pike, and parade-ground drill. In this way it was hoped that England would be better prepared for a large-scale modern war than if she still relied on the medieval feudal army and voluntary levies.

Extra care was paid to the country's defences. With the new effectiveness of big guns and artillery, it was necessary to design new types of castle walls – walls that were so massive that they could not be shot down by cannons or by mines, and which also gave the defending cannons positioned on the walls a perfect field of fire. Many new designs were put forward, which were elegantly planned in star-shapes or semicircles. Leonardo da Vinci produced several of these designs (as well as ideas for guns on wheels, like tanks) and Henry VIII used these modern plans for a chain of castles that he built to defend the ports of the south coast of England, which was particularly vulnerable to attack from foreign navies from across the channel.

The walls of medieval castles could be destroyed fairly easily by sappers, who laid a charge of several barrels of gunpowder against them. With many wars being a succession of sieges of castles or fortified towns, it was essential to devise a more effective protection.

As the wars of religion aroused new passions in the soldiers, they tended to be much more cruel than previously to the civilian population. In earlier times they had pillaged and looted; but now they massacred women and children in the name of Christ.

Infantrymen carrying pikes or halberds still formed the core of every army; they were arranged in companies of squares and marched in close formation on a battlefield. Most soldiers wore a breast-plate and helmet as armour; but some only had leather jackets for protection. The knights and commanders still had heavy, full armour, but it became less popular as it gave little protection against bullets, and was too cumbersome. The knights developed a new tactic – using pistols during a mass cavalry charge on the enemy infantry.

Charles V, the Holy Roman Emperor, himself commanded his armies in a successful siege on the Turkish fortress of Tunis in 1535. The army pitched camp on the beach in front of the fortress, and Charles took up residence in the large, red and gold tent.

War at sea became increasingly important, especially for England. Henry VIII built the first large warship, called the *Henri Grace à Dieu*. Previously, sea-battles had involved boarding enemy ships; now they took the form of cannonades and outmanoeuvring the enemy.

# The Court and Country Houses

**The courts of the kings and queens of Europe were more luxurious and more expensive than ever before.** The rulers tried to show off their magnificence in lavishness, learning and sport – while their courtiers acquired the new arts expected of them – poetry, dancing and singing. Even the oldfashioned pursuits of the kings and the nobility, such as jousting and hunting, were now treated with new elegance and refinement. When Elizabeth, for instance, went hunting, much of the expedition was taken up with a magnificent picnic.

The price of all this new splendour was a severe burden on the country's taxation. Thomas Cromwell regularly complained about the cost of the building programmes of his king, Henry VIII. One way of saving money, much used by Elizabeth, was to take herself and her entire court on a regular tour of the kingdom, and stay with the nobles or other great men on the way. Many of her hosts tried to provide luxury as fine as that available in Westminster, and ruined themselves in the process.

Now the great age of building country houses began. There were no more private castles built; instead of draughty buildings with thick walls and tiny windows, people built houses with far more glass, far more furniture, and more comfortable living quarters. For the first time, it became common to put carpets on the floor instead of rushes; picture galleries were introduced, and the kitchens were built away from the great hall.

In England, the first of these great houses was Hampton Court, built by Thomas Wolsey and later taken over by Henry VIII. However, the dissolution of the monasteries preceded a spate of country house building. These great houses were financed from the wealth of the monastic estates and the materials for them came from the great abbeys which were pulled down and destroyed. Longleat is an example of an Elizabethan palace which was built during this period.

'Real tennis' was a favourite game of kings; Henry VIII prided himself on his skill at it. The game is played indoors on a special court, and the ball is allowed to hit the walls and even the roof of the spectators' gallery. A form of it can still be seen at Hampton Court.

Hunting was popular with the wealthy. In England the main prey was boar and deer, but in central Europe the more dangerous sport of hunting bears with spears was popular. Bear-baiting, when a bear was set against mastiffs, was a star attraction in fairs.

The new refinement of the courts improved table manners. Forks were used for the first time (though they did not become common in England until the 1660s) and magnificent sets of cutlery and plate were made. Many people kept all their fortune in this 'plate'.

Dancing was a special accomplishment of the royal courts; the popular dances were the stately pavane and the more lively galliard. Masked balls were always a favourite at the English court, where the masks hid the identity of the dancers.

The kings of France sometimes organized mock sea-battles in the grounds of their castle for the amusement of the court. The idea came from the Romans, who used to flood their amphitheatres for such fights. In this illustration, the Christians are fighting with the Turks, in galleys like those

which were common in the eastern Mediterranean. For this battle, all the sailors were actually members of the royal army, and few real casualties were suffered. But such battles were not far from reality; the Turks still dominated the eastern Mediterranean.

# Fun and Games

**Life was not all hard work, war and politics.** More perhaps than any other period in history, men and women of the 16th century knew how to enjoy themselves. Rich and poor both had their entertainments and their games, which were energetic, unrestrained and sometimes violent. Almost everyone joined in – all but a few religious fanatics, people who said that it was a sin to enjoy yourself. The rest of the population hated these 'killjoys'; Shakespeare, for instance, caricatures one such puritan, in the character of Malvolio, in his play *Twelfth Night*. For the rest, there were inns and bawdy houses where wine, women and song could all be had as well as gambling, on cards, dice and backgammon; there were special arenas to enjoy the cruelty of cock-fighting, or bear-baiting; there were sports like archery, a primitive kind of football and wrestling; and, especially in London, there was the theatre. In Elizabeth's reign, the first public theatres opened, and the plays of Shakespeare, Jonson and Marlowe were huge successes with people of every class and background. Their plays combined the popular and the refined, slapstick and art, in just the right proportions for the audience to enjoy.

Above all, the 16th century was an age of showing off; of bright clothes, magnificent processions, and festivals or masques that were meant to entrance the spectator by their magnificence and the magic of their staging. Everyone enjoyed processions and demonstrations of generosity from the rich; and everyone found a simple pleasure in meeting the unusual, the curious or the grotesque. Thus kings gave each other elephants, rhinoceroses and ostriches, and Leonardo sketched the most ugly and distorted faces he could find. Thus, too, princes organized festivals of incredible splendour for their people, sometimes for days on end, to celebrate their latest diplomatic achievement or victory in war. In the processions of soldiers dressed in their traditional uniform, the people could see their pride in their homeland, the greatness of its past and of its future, and at the same time see the force which protected them from foreign aggressors.

Florence experienced some spectacular festivals given by the Medici family. The fountains ran with wine, and the town was lit by fireworks, some of the earliest of their kind to be seen in Europe. On one occasion, 300 oxen were killed for a public feast.

Cockfighting, with specially trained birds armed with metal talons on their claws, won great popularity in England in Elizabeth's reign. People enjoyed betting on the fights. Bear-baiting, in which a bear, tied to a post, was attacked by mastiffs, was also much enjoyed.

The Globe Theatre, in London, was the home of Shakespeare's theatre company. The plays were performed in the open air, with little scenery. Rich or important members of the audience sat right on the stage, others sat or stood around in the various galleries.

Many towns in Europe, especially on the Mediterranean, celebrated the 'carnival' as one of their largest and most popular festivals. Held on Shrove Tuesday just before Lent, there were processions with floats and people dressed in amazing costumes, representing mythical animals or famous people. They all did honour to the 'King Carnival'. Sometimes the carnival was an occasion for political unrest; more often, it was a time of great bawdiness and drunkenness, when all the people tried to enjoy themselves to the full.

# Postscript

Between 1450 and 1600, many things were discovered and much was achieved. But few of these discoveries and achievements had hardened into their final form by 1600. It is true that South America had already been parcelled up between Spain and Portugal; but in the rest of the world, discovery had only occasionally been followed up by colonization. The empires of the Europeans were still made up only of small outposts with trading rights; they were not vast expanses of conquered territories, ruled over by great armies. In the Far East, Europeans traded, and made themselves extremely rich; but they only took control of a few ports or islands that seemed to be vital to their trade. In North America, the rivers and coasts of the eastern seaboard were well known to explorers, but they were still un-colonized, and much of the land had not even yet been claimed by any European power. It was not until the 17th century, when the English, French and Dutch all managed to set up permanent colonies there, that the history of modern North America really began to take shape. Africa, too, was largely unknown, except for a few trading posts, and as a source for slaves. Europeans had penetrated India, China and Japan, and traded with them all on equal terms; but there was still no question of Europeans trying to force their culture onto these ancient civilizations by war.

In the same way many of the problems raised by the intellectual and political developments in Europe itself remained to be sorted out in the future. The most urgent was religion. The wars of religion had reached a lull by 1600, but less than twenty years later they broke out once more into a war that would be Europe's largest and bloodiest conflict until the 20th century. The monarchs of Europe's great nations, especially Spain and England, had managed to build up an awesome authority, far greater than that of their predecessors; and yet, even in these same countries, the growing prosperity of the people soon brought the middle classes into direct, and sometimes violent conflict with their monarchs. In England, this conflict led to the execution of Charles I by Oliver Cromwell. In many countries new industries had developed and new machines invented to be used in them; but for the next 150 years, these industries still produced far less than they could have done, because they were still dependent on water and wind for their source of power. These industries, which could have solved the problems caused by growing population, growing unemployment and rising prices, were shackled by their own inefficiency.

What was perhaps Europe's biggest discovery of all in the 16th century, the discovery of the possibility of questioning authority, thinking for one's self and practising whatever religion one pleased, had become firmly rooted by 1600; but its final victories were still a long way off. In most countries it was to be at least another century before liberty of conscience, freedom of the press, and their logical developments, political liberty and even democracy, had finally defeated the voices of hierarchy and authority. In England and the Netherlands these were assured by 1700; France had to wait until the Revolution of 1789.

But the way was open to the future, and it was in the resolution of all these conflicts that the world in which we live today was created. And it is for this reason that the 16th century is rightly known as the beginning of the modern age, and the era of discovery.

# Time Chart

|  |  |
|------|-------|
| 1453 | The Turks capture Constantinople |
| 1454 | Gutenburg invents printing |
| 1455 | Start of the Wars of the Roses |
| 1456 | The first Bible printed, at Mainz |
| 1456 | William Caxton sets up the first English printing press |
| 1478 | The Spanish Inquisition set up |
| 1478 | Bartholomew Diaz sails round the Cape of Good Hope |
| 1485 | Henry VII (Henry Tudor) wins the English throne |
| 1492 | The reconquest of Spain from the Moors completed |
| 1492 | Christopher Columbus discovers Cuba and the Bahamas |
| 1494 | The world beyond Europe divided between Spain and Portugal |
| 1495 | Charles VIII of France starts the Italian Wars |
| 1497 | John Cabot discovers Newfoundland |
| 1498 | Vasco da Gama reaches India |
| 1498 | The monk Savonarola has a brief spell of power in Florence |
| 1503–06 | Leonardo da Vinci paints the *Mona Lisa* |
| 1504 | Michelangelo sculpts *David* |
| 1509 | Accession of Henry VIII in England |
| 1513 | Scottish army entirely destroyed by the English at Flodden |
| 1515 | Accession of Francis I in France |
| 1515 | The French win an important victory at Marignano |
| 1516 | Thomas More writes *Utopia* |
| 1519 | Charles V becomes Holy Roman Emperor |
| 1519–21 | Hernan Cortès conquers Mexico |
| 1520 | Henry VIII and Francis I meet at the Field of the Cloth of Gold |
| 1521 | Ferdinand Magellan returns from sailing around the world |
| 1520 | The Portuguese reach China |
| 1521 | Martin Luther states the basis of the Protestant faith |
| 1525 | Charles V beats Francis I at Pavia |
| 1525 | The Peasants' War in the Empire |
| 1526 | Hans Holbein comes to England |
| 1527 | Rome is sacked by the armies of Charles V |
| 1527 | The Medici family driven out of Florence |
| 1529 | Fall of Thomas Wolsey from power in England |
| 1532 | Niccolo Machiavelli writes *The Prince* |
| 1533 | Henry VIII divorces Catherine of Aragon |
| 1534 | Henry VIII declares himself head of the English Church |
| 1534 | Francisco Pizarro conquers Peru |
| 1536 | Wales formally united with England |
| 1536 | Henry VIII and Thomas Cromwell suppress the English monasteries |
| 1540 | Fall of Thomas Cromwell from power |
| 1541 | Jean Calvin sets up a puritan state in Geneva |
| 1542 | The Portuguese reach Japan |
| 1543 | Vesalius publishes his studies of human anatomy |
| 1543 | Copernicus argues that the universe revolves around the sun |
| 1545 | The Catholics begin the Counter-Reformation |
| 1547 | Accession of Edward VI in England |
| 1549 | English Book of Common Prayer published |
| 1549 | Rebellion of the Cornishmen |
| 1553 | Accession of Mary in England |
| 1555 | Abdication of Charles V |
| 1556 | Execution of Thomas Cranmer |
| 1556 | Agricola publishes his study of metallurgy |
| 1558 | Accession of Elizabeth I in England |
| 1560 | Protestantism set up in Scotland |
| 1561 | Accession of Mary Queen of Scots |
| 1562 | John Hawkins takes slaves from Africa to the New World |
| 1568 | Start of the Dutch revolt against the Spaniards |
| 1568 | Mary Queen of Scots driven out of Scotland |
| 1568 | Mercator publishes his map of the world |
| 1571 | The Turkish fleet defeated at Lepanto |
| 1572 | Start of the French Wars of Religion |
| 1577–80 | Francis Drake sails around the world |
| 1585 | Walter Raleigh tries to set up a colony in Virginia |
| 1587 | Mary Queen of Scots executed |
| 1588 | England defeats the Spanish Armada |
| 1589 | Accession of Henry IV of France |
| 1590 | William Shakespeare's first plays performed |
| 1597 | Galileo Galilei studying astronomy |
| 1598 | End of the French Wars of Religion |
| 1601 | The English Poor Law enacted |
| 1603 | Accession of James VI of Scotland to become James I of England |

# A Renaissance View of Animals

*'And as for a knowledge of nature, I want you to devote yourself to it carefully; I want you to know the fish in every sea, river and stream, every bird of the airs, every tree, shrub and bush of the forests, every plant, every metal hidden in the heart of the mountains, every stone of the East and the South. There will be nothing that you will be unable to recognize.'*

Letter from Gargantua to his son Pantagruel. Rabelais, *Pantagruel*, chapter VIII. 1532.

## Lorraine 1505

King René II of Lorraine kept two civets at his ducal palace in Nancy. These animals were remarkable for the double pouch under their tails, which contained a substance that was said to improve fertility and give people a large family. All you had to do was spray your room with it to feel the effects. The King kept a fire burning day and night in the civets' room, and had a bed made for them out of two boxes covered in grey cloth and filled with cushions. On 31 December, the palace housekeeper presented the account of the food the civets had consumed since the previous 20 September: 135 lamb joints, 6 chickens, 3 pullets, veal and mutton fat, rice and candles. The King was surprised to find that such small animals had such large appetites. His grandfather, René the Good, had also had a civet, for which Jean Bidet of Angers was made Keeper of the King of Sicily's Civet. His treasurer gave him just 16 sous with which to feed and keep warm the animal for a whole month. Perhaps this civet had less of an appetite than René II's?

## Rome 1500

It is said that a cardinal paid a sailor a hundred gold pieces for a grey African parrot that could recite the Apostles' Creed perfectly.

## Spain 1504

One of the companions of Christopher Columbus claimed that the American Indians captured turtles with the help of a curious sucking fish which they called a remora.

## The Netherlands 1504

Jeanne the Mad, wife of prince Philip I, used to keep several bears in her home at Ghent.

## England 1506

Thomas Blundeville published the fourth part of his encyclopedic work on horses' illnesses.

## The Netherlands 1510

Margaret of Austria, the governor of the Netherlands, kept three civets at her palace at Ghent. They were her pride and joy; she took them with her on her travels, walked them in her gardens, and held them in her arms even when she was wearing a dress with wide sleeves edged with ermine.

## France 1510

Louis XII gave the gentlemen of his household a crow that he had trained to hunt pheasants.

## Rome 1514

Manuel I, king of Portugal, sent the explorer Tristan da Cunha as an ambassador to Rome to honour the election of Pope Leo X, one of the Medici family. The ambassador entered the Eternal City on 12 March, followed by an extraordinary train that included an elephant. When the beast arrived under the windows of the Holy Palace, it stopped to bow three times on the order of its driver. It then caught sight of a large tank full of water; it plunged its trunk in and sprayed the assembled company, without respect even for the person of the Holy Father himself. Luckily the Pope was greatly amused, and gave orders for the elephant to be installed in the Vatican. Painters were sent to paint its portrait; Beroalde the Younger even composed a poem in its honour. The animal was decked out in gold, and gave Garabello de Gaeto, another poet, a ride up to the Capitol.

### France 1516
In the region of Villenauxe, in the Champagne area, the vines suffered from an unusual parasite. The ecclesiastical judge from the city of Troyes told the people to repent of their sins and then gave the parasites six days to leave the region, on pain of eternal damnation and excommunication.

### Poland 1517
Several aurochs, or prehistoric oxen, were seen in the forests near Warsaw by the Austrian baron Herberstein.

### France 1517
A Portuguese ship, captained by Jan da Pinho, tied up at Marseilles in October 1517; on board was a rhinoceros, another present for Pope Leo X from the king of Portugal. Francis I, the French king, asked da Pinha to disembark the animal so that the townspeople could see it. The captain then presented the king with a magnificent horse and harness to match, and Francis gave him 5,000 gold crowns in thanks. In December the ship sailed on towards Rome, but it was caught in a storm off Genoa and was lost with all hands. The body of the rhinoceros was retrieved, and was stuffed and then sent to Rome. The artist Albrecht Dürer did an engraving of it.

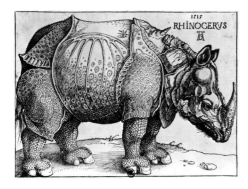

### Portugal 1517
The king of Portugal was very interested in strange animals and he decided to solve the question that had been occupying his courtiers. Everyone wanted to know whether elephants and rhinoceroses hated each other. The king ordered the streets of Lisbon to be cleared. He then had an elephant and a rhinoceros brought face to face. The elephant took one look at the rhinoceros, threw his rider and fled for the safety of his stable, trumpeting with fear all the way.

### Rome 1523
A pair of turkeys arrived in the Vatican, a present from the archbishop of San Domingo to Pope Clement VII. These birds were common in the New World, but this was the first pair to be seen in Europe.

### France 1526
Francis I created four new offices for looking after all his birds. They were the Captain of the Great Aviary, the Master of the Singing Birds, the Feeder of the Nightingale, and the Governor of the Canaries.

### England 1530
A Portuguese boat which tied up at Plymouth had on board about thirty large ducks from the Gold Coast of Africa, known as Barbary ducks. Actually, these animals were not native to those parts of Africa, but had been taken there from Peru by slave traders. Some people were allowed to try their flesh; they decided to try breeding them themselves.

### France 1531
The bishop of Auxerre had one of his attendants crucified after he was found guilty of stealing two falcons. Later, the bishop himself was sentenced to solitary confinement for life.

### Lyon, France 1531
M. Chassanée, the mayor of the town, published a book known as his *Advice*. The first chapter, which is two hundred and fifty-six paragraphs long, is a commentary on ways of dealing with insects and other nuisances.

### Spain 1528
The conquistador Francisco Pizarro returned from the New World in the spring, and was received by Charles V. He showed the emperor some small golden drinking vessels, in the shape of a curious animal something like a small camel. The Incas called them llamas. They were used as beasts of burden, carrying up to 45 kilos, and their meat was also tasty. The Incas also kept a similar animal called an alpaca. Its beautiful wool was spun by the women and turned into fine cloth.

### Rome 1533
*Hippiatrica sive Marescalia*, a book written in 1486 by Laurentius Rusus, an Italian expert on horses, was now translated into French. It was full of information on how to train horses by using iron bars with sharp hooks, whips and spurs. It also explained how to cure a horse of restlessness – by applying a redhot branding-iron under the tail. It seems that all the author expected a groom to know was how to shoe his horses, and not to be able to feed and care for them.

### New France 1535

The French explorer Jacques Cartier travelled up the St Lawrence river in Canada, as far as present-day Quebec and Montreal. There he heard tell of beavers, roe-deer and turtledoves, all living in great numbers in those parts. He thought that all these were similar to the species found in the Old World.

### Flanders 1536

The Emperor Charles V paid 120 livres for a lion, which he kept at Ghent. It was to be a companion for the three other animals which he had obtained in Tunis and sent to Flanders via Naples.

### France 1543

The elders of the city of Geneva asked that the slugs which were infesting their fields be excommunicated.

### France 1545

The chief falconer of Francis I at this time was in charge of fifty gentleman falconers and fifty assistants. There were 300 birds in the royal falconry, and they cost 4,000 florins a year to keep.

### Germany 1546

At Oppenheim, on the river Rhine, a pig killed a child and ate it. The pig was later buried alive in punishment.

### France 1547

Three Italian riding-masters, Federico Grisone and Batista Pignatelli from Naples, and Cesare Fiaschi from Florence, opened a riding school in Paris.

### France 1550

When Henry II and his queen, Catherine de Medici, made their triumphal entry into Rouen, they had a dromedary and some elephants. The King kept these and other exotic animals at St Germain; they had been sent to him by Pierre Gilles, the agent for the previous king Francis I.

### France 1551

When Mary Queen of Scots was living at Blois as queen of France, she had her own zoo with her. Its attendant was allowed five pence a day to cover the cost of food. There were dogs, including bulldogs, horses large and small, including Mary's two riding-horses Bravanne and Madame la Réale. There were some bears too, but these caused so much damage that the woman looking after them had to be paid off.

### Hungary 1552

Maximilian II, the Hapsburg king of Bohemia and Hungary, held a festival in May to celebrate his coronation. In the procession was an elephant which he had brought from Spain the previous year, and which was living at his castle of Ebersdorf, near Vienna.

Earlier in the year, in January, travellers from Austria claimed to have seen this same elephant in the courtyard of an inn at Brixen, near Innsbruck. The inn-keeper changed the name of the inn to *Zum Elephanten* – a name it bears to this day.

### England 1560

Some townsmen from Flanders arrived at Dover, trying to escape from the Spanish soldiers. They brought with them some canaries; it was the first time that these songbirds had been seen in England.

### France 1565

Charles IX presented his mother Catherine with 100 kilos of whales' tongues, preserved in salt. This meat was considered a great delicacy.

### Rome 1567

In a Papal Bull of 1 November 1567, Pope Pius V threatened with excommunication any king or any priest who organized a bullfight. He also decreed that any man killed in a bullfight should be refused a Christian burial.

## France 1569

Bezoar, which is a substance like stone and found in the stomachs of cows, had been thought by apothecaries to be capable of producing miraculous cures for many ailments, including plague, epilepsy, vertigo and poisoning. But now the French king outlawed the substance and ordered all remaining supplies to be burnt. His surgeon Ambroise Paré had made an experiment with it: he had given some poison to a man already condemned to death, and then given him some bezoar to see if it would really cure him. It did not work, and the man died. Bezoar had also been obtained from llamas; Spanish merchants had made a fortune out of their trade in it.

## England 1569

About 300 refugees from the Spanish Netherlands had settled in Norwich; they introduced a new sport which they played every Sunday and which soon became popular with the English. It was cockfighting; the cocks had their crests cut and long sharp knives attached to their claws. The craze for cockfighting began in Peru and Mexico, among the Spanish troops there; they brought it back to Europe, and introduced it to the Netherlands. In England, even Queen Elizabeth took great pleasure in the sport, and kept her own trained cocks.

## Russia 1570

The tsar Ivan the Terrible was said to use hungry bears to torture his enemies, or anyone else who defied his orders. Some travellers declared that Russia was so barbarous that the peasants were not at all afraid of wolves; on some evenings they amused themselves by howling in reply to the wolves.

## France 1571

When Charles IX married Elizabeth of Austria, there was a great banquet and turkeys were eaten. This was the first occasion on which anyone in France had tasted their meat.

## France 1572

A solemn festival was held in Paris to celebrate the feast of St John, on 23 June. Charles IX, using a candle made from white wax weighing a kilo, lit a great bonfire. Cats tied up in sacks, were thrown onto it, and this year a fox was thrown onto the pyre as well to delight the king.

## Lorraine 1572

At Moyenmoutier, in the Vosges mountains, a pig was found eating a child. It was taken to prison and locked up under the name of Claudon, its owner. Legal proceedings began at Nancy, the capital of Lorraine; eventually the council of aldermen declared that the pig Claudon was to be 'hanged and strangled; it must be tied up with a rope, completely naked because it is only a rude beast.'

## The Netherlands 1573

When besieged by the Spaniards, the people of Haarlem received a message by pigeon. It was from their commander William of Orange, saying that reinforcements and provisions were on their way.

## Germany 1577

Louis IV, landgrave of Hesse, issued a law that anyone who caught falcons or robbed their nests was liable for imprisonment.

## Spain 1580

About 64 kilos of cochineals, small insects that live on a special cactus in Mexico, were sent to Spain. When they were boiled, dried and ground up, they were dissolved in a solution of sodium bicarbonate and alum. A scarlet lacquer resulted, which was used to dye cloth.

## France 1583

The town of Embrun, in Provence, was sacked by Calvinist troops in the French Wars of Religion. The Calvinist commander wanted to ride on horseback into the Catholic church – but his horse, seized with miraculous fear, reared up at the last minute and refused to take part in the sacrilege of his master.

## Artois 1585

Another pig killed a child, this time at Saint-Omer.

## France 1585

When the region of Valence was infested with caterpillars, the head of the ecclesiastical court invoked solemn curses. They worked extremely well.

### Savoy 1587

When a particular type of weevil was found to be causing havoc in the vineyards of Saint-Julien, a case was taken to court. The weevils were assigned a lawyer and a barrister, and the case was heard properly. The judge decided that the villagers should set aside one field for the weevils to live in. They chose one, and drew up a lease for the field in favour of the weevils, which were to have full legal rights over the field for perpetuity.

### Saint Helena 1588

On this small Atlantic island, a few oak trees, planted in 1513, were found growing in the dense forest. Today there are several thousand oaks on the island.

### Navarre 1588

On 12 June, King Henry paid 100 crowns for a hat decorated with an amethyst and topped with several white ostrich feathers.

### France 1590

When Henry IV was besieging Paris, the defenders sent out their offer of surrender by pigeon.

### Rome 1590

Pope Gregory XIV was sent a rhinoceros horn from Asia. He put it in a leather sheath; his doctors advised him to take a small portion of it, powdered up, in the hopes of curing his chronic ailments.

### France 1591

When he was besieging the town of Noyon, Henry IV heard that an elephant had arrived for him at Dieppe from the East Indies. Henry kept it at Dieppe, since the menagerie that he took with him on his campaigns was already large enough. It consisted of a large monkey called Robert; a smaller monkey; a large orange ape and a small black one; and a parrot. All these animals were kept in a cage and carried on the back of a horse which was looked after by the Secretary of the King's Council.

### France 1595

A wolf swam across the Seine and killed a child in the centre of Paris.

### Marseilles, France 1596

A school of dolphins swam into the harbour and blocked the shipping lanes. A cardinal sent the bishop to exorcise the animals with holy water. As a result they swam off into the high seas once more.

### France 1598

Antoine du Pluviel was made master of the King's Great Stables by Henry IV. He had once been a pupil of the Italian master Battista Pignatelli.

### Venice 1598

After the death of the noble lord, Carlo Ruini, a senator of Bologna, his son Ottavio published a monumental book written by his father, called *Anatomia del Cavallo, infermita et suoi remedii* (the anatomy of the horse, its diseases and their cures). The book was illustrated with fine plates, in both black-and-white and colour – obviously the work of a master who was equally at home with a scalpel and a pencil. Everyone was amazed; especially those who had seen the sketches that Leonardo da Vinci had done for his equestrian statue of Francisco Sforza at Milan. The surface muscles in these sketches were identical with those in the woodcuts of *Anatomia del Cavallo*. This made people wonder who really did them.

### France 1600

Henry IV ordered that 20,000 mulberry trees be planted at the Tuileries; he was hoping that they would assist the growth of the French silk industry.

# The Strange Beasts of Francis I of France

When the King of France decided to ally himself with the Turks against the power of Charles V, the ambassadors he sent to Constantinople came back laden with a number of strange beasts.

One of these ambassadors, Pierre Pitou, took with him 1,400 livres to buy animals for the King; in 1533 he brought back four camels with him. These were taken to the King, who sent them to Avignon where the Pope could see them. Pitou also bought some ostriches; their fine feathers were used to decorate the King's hats. He kept these ostriches in his private gardens.

Mary of Hungary, the regent of the Netherlands, sent Francis two seals from Brussels in 1539 together with a barrel of malmsey wine and several other bottles of Hungarian wine. The Queen of France received these gifts when she was staying at the abbey of Valusan near Troyes. She left them in the safekeeping of the monks, and sent some Languedoc wine to Mary in thanks.

Francis himself sometimes allowed a lion, as big as an ox, to sleep in his bedroom with him; at other times he would have a bear or a leopard in his bedroom. When he went hunting he often took a cheetah, which an attendant carried on a cushion behind his saddle. This cheetah was quite unequalled at hunting hares; it caught and strangled them in a moment.

# Index